★ THE CIVIL WAR ★

A NATION
DIVIDED

The Long Road to the Civil War

By Don Nardo

Content Adviser: Brett Barker, PhD,
Assistant Professor of History,
University of Wisconsin–Marathon County

Reading Adviser: Alexa L. Sandmann, EdD, Professor of Literacy,
College and Graduate School of Education, Health, and
Human Services, Kent State University

COMPASS POINT BOOKS
a capstone imprint

Compass Point Books
151 Good Counsel Drive
P.O. Box 669
Mankato, MN 56002-0669

This book was manufactured with paper containing
at least 10 percent post-consumer waste.

Managing Editor: Catherine Neitge
Designer: Heidi Thompson
Media Researcher: Svetlana Zhurkin
Library Consultant: Kathleen Baxter
Production Specialist: Jane Klenk
Cartographer: XNR Productions, Inc.

Library of Congress Cataloging-in-Publication Data
Nardo, Don, 1947–
 A nation divided : the long road to the Civil War / by Don Nardo.
   p. cm.—(The Civil War)
 Includes bibliographical references and index.
 ISBN 978-0-7565-4367-9 (library binding)
 ISBN 978-0-7565-4412-6 (paperback)
1. United States—History—Civil War, 1861–1865—Causes—Juvenile
literature. 2. Slavery—Southern States—History—Juvenile literature.
3. United States—Politics and government—1849–1861—Juvenile
literature. 4. Southern States—Politics and government—1775–1865—Juvenile literature.
I. Title. II. Series.
 E459.N37 2010
 973.7'11—dc22   2010001016

Visit Compass Point Books on the Internet at *www.capstonepub.com*

TABLE OF CONTENTS

CHAPTER 1
TWO SEPARATE WORLDS

The American Civil War is the most devastating conflict the United States has ever fought. More than 620,000 people were killed or mortally wounded in battle or died of disease during the war. That's almost as many as the number of Americans killed in all the country's other wars put together! Many others were maimed for life. The conflict made untold thousands of people homeless and spread misery and hatred throughout the land.

The Civil War began in 1861. That was the year that Abraham Lincoln became the nation's 16th president. The war ended in 1865, the year he was struck down by an assassin. During those years Lincoln was the commander in chief of the Union, often called the North. Opposing the Union in the war was the Confederacy. Often called the South, it was composed of the states that seceded from the country in 1860 and 1861.

★ECONOMIC DEPENDENCE

The outbreak of war between these two regions of the United States was not a sudden, unexpected event. It occurred after decades of important, and in some cases profound, differences between them. Some differences were economic. Others were cultural or moral. Whatever their nature, by the late 1850s they had caused the North and South to become largely separate societies. They were so distinct, in fact, that it was common for people on one side to mock or belittle those on the other. In 1860, for example, a Georgia lawyer insulted Yankees, the common southern term for northerners. The two groups, he said, "could no more mix than oil and water. They have been so entirely separated by climate, by morals, by religion, and by estimates so totally opposite of all that constitutes honor, truth, and manliness, that they cannot longer exist under the same government."

In contrast, as a modern observer

Southerners and most northerners had very different attitudes about the enslavement of blacks.

puts it, many northerners saw southerners as "an alien people economically and socially degraded."

One major reason for this mutual dislike was a difference in lifestyle between northerners and southerners. By the late 1850s, more than a quarter of northerners lived in cities. Many more dwelled in good-sized towns. The North had also built up a great deal of industry. There were 1.3 million factory workers in the North, but only 110,000 in the South. As a result, northerners made 90 percent of the country's manufactured goods.

In the South, 90 percent of people lived in the countryside. More than 80 percent of them worked in agriculture. In addition, a large majority of southerners were poor or nearly so. A few, though, were wealthy plantation owners. They grew cotton and other crops and depended heavily on slave labor.

Because of these differences, the South had become, in many ways, economically dependent on the North. Many southerners deeply resented the situation.

"We purchase all our luxuries and necessaries from the North," a southern newspaper complained. "Our slaves are clothed with Northern manufactured goods [and] work with Northern hoes, ploughs, and other implements. The slaveholder dresses in Northern goods, rides in a Northern saddle … [and] reads Northern books. … [He writes] on Northern-made paper, with

Four slave-holding border states—Delaware, Kentucky, Maryland, and Missouri—remained loyal to the North during the Civil War.

a Northern pen, with Northern ink. … In Northern vessels his products are carried to market."

Some southerners felt disgraced by their economic dependence on the North. Particularly vocal on the issue was New Orleans magazine editor James B.D. De Bow. In 1852 he estimated that northern dominance in business cost southerners $100 million per year, the same as about $2.6 billion today. "Great God!" he thundered in his magazine. "Will we not throw off this humiliating dependence?" What was needed, he said, was "action! ACTION!! ACTION!!!" Many southerners agreed with De Bow, but the vast majority were unsure of what specific "action" they could take.

★SHARPLY CONTRASTING VIEWS

Another way the North and South had become, in a very real sense, separate worlds was in education. In the 1850s almost half of all southerners could neither read nor write. In comparison, only one in 20 northerners was illiterate. Only half as many southerners regularly went to school as New Englanders did. This was mainly because every northern state had a free public school system by 1860, whereas no such systems existed in the South. Southern children were taught by tutors or attended expensive private schools. Moreover, the South turned out half as many teachers and doctors and one-sixth as many engineers as the North.

Northerners felt that their educational advantages made the North more advanced and civilized than the South. A typical northern view of southerners was expressed by a *New York Times* correspondent, Frederick Law Olmsted. He later became famous as a landscape architect and designed Central Park in New York City. After a trip through the South in the 1850s, he wrote:

"The Southerner cares for the end only; he is impatient of the means [of getting to that end]. ... But he has much less curiosity than the Northerner; less originating genius, less inventive talent, less patient and persevering energy. And I think this all comes from his [lack] of aptitude for close observation and his dislike for application to small

Not until the end of the 1800s were all children in the U.S. guaranteed a public elementary school education.

details. And this, I think, may be reasonably supposed to be mainly the result of habitually leaving [a large part of his work] to his slaves."

Many people in the South saw the situation as just the opposite. In their view, it was the Yankees who were less civilized. A common opinion of southerners was that the North was overpopulated and crime-ridden. They also believed northerners tended to be less decent and less honest than southerners, who were kinder and more honorable. People in the South, a Virginia lawyer and social commentator, George

Southerners often held an unrealistic view of country life.

Fitzhugh, wrote in 1854, were peaceful and contented.
"We have no mobs," he said, "no trades unions, no
strikes for higher wages, no armed resistance to the
law, but little jealousy of the rich by the poor. We have
but few in our jails, and fewer in our poor houses. …
We are wholly exempt from the torrent of [poverty
and crime that exists in] the already crowded North.
… Money is, with few exceptions, the only thing that
ennobles at the North. We have poor among us, but
none who are over-worked and under fed. We do not
crowd cities because lands are abundant and their

SOUTHERN "SUPERIORITY"

Southern lawyer George Fitzhugh argued in 1854 that southerners were more refined and respectable than northerners:

"Our society exhibits no appearance of precocity [maturing too early], no symptoms of decay. A long course of continuing improvement is in prospect before us. ... Actual liberty and equality with our white population has been approached much nearer than in the free States. Few of our whites ever work as day laborers, none as cooks, ... body servants, or in other menial capacities. One free citizen does not lord it over another; hence that feeling of independence and equality that distinguishes us; hence that pride of character, that self-respect, that gives us ascendancy [superiority] when we come in contact with Northerners. It is a distinction to be a Southerner, as it was once to be a Roman citizen."

owners kind, merciful and hospitable." Fitzhugh's views, of course, were highly biased and distorted. He was a white person describing the feelings of fellow whites in a society in which black people were enslaved—hardly a merciful or hospitable situation.

★AMERICANS AS ENEMIES

Whether these supposed differences between northerners and southerners were real or not, their unflattering views of each other meant trouble for the nation's future. More and more, each side came to dislike and distrust the other. Many southerners became convinced that northerners wanted to destroy the South's culture and way of life. So the North was the South's enemy. This dangerous concept—of Americans' seeing one another as enemies—also existed in the North. Massachusetts

NORTHERN FOE

A Massachusetts minister, Theodore Parker, penned this scathing attack on southern culture in 1854:

"The South—I must say it—is the enemy of the North. She is the foe to Northern industry—to our mines, our manufactures, and our commerce. ... She is the foe to our institutions—to our democratic politics in the State, our democratic culture in the school, our democratic work in the community, our democratic equality in the family, and our democratic religion in the Church. ... England is the rival of the North, a powerful rival, often dangerous. ... But the South is our foe, far more dangerous, meaner, and more dishonorable."

Slavery existed in America for hundreds of years before it sparked the bloody Civil War.

clergyman Theodore Parker called the South "the enemy of our material welfare and our spiritual development." He added, "Her success is our ruin."

Yet even such widespread misunderstanding and hatred between North and South were not enough to provoke all-out war. It was one specific issue—slavery— that ended up doing that. The South's economy and culture, in many ways, were supported by slavery. And when that institution seemed threatened, many southerners felt it was time to fight.

CHAPTER 2
THE CRITICAL ISSUE
OF SLAVERY

Most modern historians agree that slavery was the main cause of the American Civil War. Economic, political, cultural, and other differences had made the North and South two separate societies or civilizations. But southern slavery caused or reinforced many of the differences. And more than any other single issue, it continued to drive the two societies apart. A southern newspaper, the *Charleston Mercury*, concisely summed it up in 1858. "On the subject of slavery," it said, "the North and South … are not only two Peoples, but they are rival, hostile Peoples."

It was not simply that slavery was an institution in the South that caused the trouble. It was that southerners sought to expand that institution into other states and territories. On this point, many northerners drew a line in the sand. As a leading northern politician, William H. Seward, put it, a collision between free labor and the spread of slavery was inevitable. That collision, he said, "is an irrepressible conflict between opposing and enduring forces; and it means that the United States must and will, sooner or later, become either entirely a slave-holding nation, or entirely a free-labor nation. It is the failure to apprehend this great truth, that induces so many unsuccessful attempts at final compromise between the slave and free States."

William H. Seward served as governor of New York, senator from New York, and U.S. secretary of state.

★ DEFENDERS OF SLAVERY

One reason southern whites defended slavery so fiercely was that the South's economy was based largely on slave labor. In the 40 years before the Civil War, southern cotton production grew enormously. This made the large plantation owners in the region fabulously wealthy. "Our Cotton is the most wonderful talisman [magic charm] in the world," bragged a planter in 1853. "By its power we are transmuting [transforming] whatever we choose into whatever we

Most enslaved people in the South lived and worked on cotton plantations.

want." Five years later, another leading southerner claimed that cotton production had made the South a global economic force. "The slaveholding South is now the controlling power of the world," he said, which was an exaggeration. "No power on earth dares … to make war on cotton. Cotton is king."

These men were well aware that cotton could not have been king without the cheap labor provided by black slaves. Roughly 3.5 million enslaved people lived and worked in the South in the 1850s. All told, they were the property of fewer than one-third of southerners. But many southerners who did not own slaves benefited indirectly from slave labor. Some hoped to become

A SOUTHERNER WHO HATED SLAVERY

Not all southerners were slave owners. Although it was dangerous to speak openly about slavery in the South, a brave few opposed it. One was North Carolina farmer Hinton R. Helper, who wrote a book condemning the institution in 1860. He said in part:

"The causes which have impeded the progress and prosperity of the South, which have dwindled our commerce ... sunk a large majority of our people in galling poverty and ignorance ... disgraced us in the recesses of our own souls, and brought us under reproach in the eyes of all civilized and enlightened nations—may all be traced to one common source, and there find solution in the most hateful and horrible word, that was ever incorporated into the vocabulary of human economy—Slavery!

"Reared amidst the institution of slavery, believing it to be wrong both in principle and in practice, and having seen and felt its evil influences upon individuals, communities and states, we deem it a duty, no less than a privilege, to enter our protest against it, and to use our most strenuous efforts to overturn and abolish it!"

slave owners themselves, and did. Some sold food and other products to slave plantations. And all enjoyed higher social status and a more pleasant way of life,

A Virginia slave is whipped at the order of an overseer (left). The drawing appears in abolitionist Mary Livermore's 1898 autobiography.

merely by being white rather than black. Rich slave owners warned that ending slavery would destroy the whole southern economy.

Many southerners, then, had a reason to maintain and defend slavery. Some claimed that by enslaving African blacks they had rescued them from barbarism. Because blacks belonged to an inferior race, the argument went, they were naturally primitive. Giving them food, clothes, and protection on an American plantation was doing them a kindness. Indeed, slavery's defenders typically perpetuated the popular lie that most slaves were well-treated and happy. In his 1857 tract "The Blessings of Slavery," Virginia lawyer George Fitzhugh stated:

"The negro slaves of the South are the happiest, and in some sense, the freest people in the world. The children and the aged and infirm work not at all, and yet have all the comforts and necessaries of life provided for them. They enjoy liberty, because they are oppressed neither by care or labor. The women do little hard work, and are protected from the despotism of their husbands by their masters. The negro men and stout boys work, on the average, in good weather, no more than nine hours a day. The balance of their time is spent in perfect abandon [leisure activities]."

Other pro-slavery arguments dispensed with fantasies like Fitzhugh's and cited harsher rationales. "For every master who cruelly treats his slave," congressman Daniel C. DeJarnette of Virginia declared, "there are two white men at the North who torture and murder their wives." Even if this had been true, which it was not, it would not have justified slavery in the South.

More bluntly racist was U.S. Senator James Hammond of South Carolina. "In all social systems," he said, "there must be a class to do the menial duties, to perform the drudgery of life. That is, a class requiring but a low order of intellect and but little skill. … Fortunately for the South, she found a race adapted to that purpose to her hand. A race inferior to her own … . We use them for our purpose, and call them slaves."

★A MONSTROUS INJUSTICE

There were northerners, too, who thought blacks were inferior to whites. But more northerners viewed slavery as morally wrong. The most vocal among them were the abolitionists, who denounced slavery and worked to abolish it. British and American abolitionists had already managed to shut down the Atlantic slave trade. Britain banned the shipment of Africans to the Americas in 1807. The U.S. government followed suit in 1808.

However, the millions of blacks who had already

Africans were chained below decks in slave ships heading to North America.

crossed the ocean remained enslaved in the American South. As a result, opponents of slavery kept trying to end what they realized was a vile, unjust institution. U.S. Senator William H. Seward of New York was one. In the 1850s he pointed out that slavery caused "an exhausted soil, old and decaying towns, [and] wretchedly-neglected roads" in the South. Also, he insisted, the institution was "incompatible" with all the "elements of the security, welfare, and greatness of nations."

In 1854 another opponent of slavery, Illinois lawyer Abraham Lincoln, spoke of the "monstrous injustice of slavery." He went on: "I hate it because it deprives our republican example of its just influence in the world—enables the enemies of free institutions, with plausibility, to taunt us as hypocrites—causes the real friends of freedom to doubt our sincerity."

Abraham Lincoln spoke out against slavery in a speech in Peoria, Illinois.

★THE SPREAD OF SLAVERY

Each side in the slavery debate pressed its case year after year with little effect. What finally raised the issue to a state of crisis was a series of attempts by southerners to expand slavery into the nation's western territories and newly created states. One major southern victory was the 1854 Kansas-Nebraska Act. It permitted residents to decide whether to allow slavery in the newly formed Kansas and Nebraska territories. Many northerners were outraged, because these areas had been closed to slavery since 1820 by the Missouri Compromise. Few were surprised when antislavery and pro-slavery groups in Kansas, the territory most likely to have slaves, began fighting. In May 1856 some of those who supported slavery attacked the antislavery town of Lawrence, destroying several buildings.

Hoping to prevent any growth in the number of pro-slavery settlers, concerned northern leaders pushed for creating a new political party. That party— the Republicans—began to organize in 1854. And in 1856 it nominated John C. Frémont as its candidate for the presidency. Frémont lost to Democrat James Buchanan. But the Republican Party, even though it existed only in the North, had become a permanent fixture in U.S. politics.

The pro-slavery forces scored other victories besides

The attack on Lawrence by pro-slavery groups in 1856 was part of a series of fights that became known as Bleeding Kansas.

the Kansas-Nebraska Act and the attacks in Kansas. One was the 1857 Dred Scott case. A slave born in Missouri, where slavery was legal, Scott moved with his owner to the free state of Illinois and Wisconsin Territory. Slavery was not legal in either place. So when his owner died, Scott went to court to get his freedom. The controversial case went all the way to the U.S. Supreme Court.

Most of the justices were southerners, and they denied Scott his freedom, using the argument that black people were not U.S. citizens. Blacks, the court held, were "so far inferior, that they had no rights which the white man was bound to respect." Therefore, "Dred Scott was not a citizen

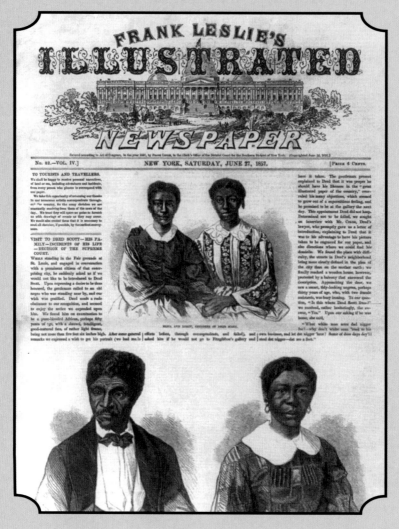

Dred Scott, his wife, Harriet, and their daughters were pictured in
Frank Leslie's Illustrated Newspaper*'s coverage of the case.*

of Missouri within the meaning of the Constitution of the
United States, and not entitled as such to sue in its courts."
The court went on to state that Congress had no power
to exclude slavery from any territory. The ruling angered
those opposed to slavery and its spread, particularly

northern Republicans, since their party had formed to halt the spread of slavery into the territories.

The antislavery forces scored their own victories in the 1850s. In 1852 *Uncle Tom's Cabin*, a book written by Harriet Beecher Stowe, a northerner, was published. A vivid account of the cruelties of slavery, it depicted a sadistic plantation owner

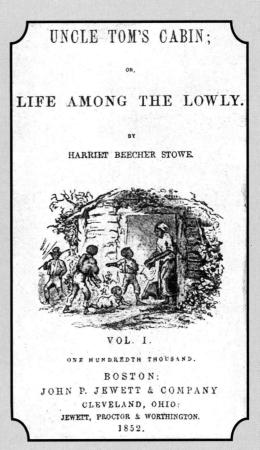

UNCLE TOM'S CABIN;

OR,

LIFE AMONG THE LOWLY.

BY

HARRIET BEECHER STOWE.

VOL. I.

ONE HUNDREDTH THOUSAND.

BOSTON:
JOHN P. JEWETT & COMPANY
CLEVELAND, OHIO:
JEWETT, PROCTOR & WORTHINGTON.
1852.

Title page from the 100,000th copy of the first edition of Uncle Tom's Cabin

having one of his slaves beaten to death. The book was a bestseller and swelled the ranks of the antislavery movement.

No less famous was a white abolitionist named John Brown. He moved to Kansas in 1855 to fight for his beliefs. On May 25, 1856, he and his followers murdered five pro-slavery settlers near Pottawatomie Creek, in eastern Kansas. Three years later Brown tried to start a slave rebellion in the South by capturing the federal armory at Harpers Ferry, Virginia, and encouraging slaves there to join his uprising. He and his followers were captured in the attempt, however. After a widely publicized trial, Brown was hanged December 2, 1859.

Despised in the South, Brown became a hero to many northerners. Some of them recalled that just before his death he had warned of much more bloodshed to come over slavery. Unfortunately for the country, these words would soon come true with a vengeance.

CHAPTER 3
THREATS OF SECESSION

Tensions between the North and South grew steadily in the 1850s. The success of Harriet Beecher Stowe's book condemning slavery in 1852, the attacks in Kansas, Dred Scott's failure to win his freedom, and John Brown's daring attack at Harpers Ferry were only a few of many incidents that inspired hatred of one side by the other.

There was one thing, however, about which people of both sides agreed—the national crisis was likely to get worse. For most southerners, worse took the form of the national election of 1860. If the Republican Party won, with its presidential candidate, Abraham Lincoln, antislavery forces would control the nation. Southern states began considering what they felt might be the only effective remedy for what they viewed as an intolerable situation: secession.

★ASSAULT IN THE SENATE

Even in the summer of 1860, secession was not yet certain. At that point, most Americans did not think that a civil war would be inevitable if the South left the Union. In fact, many southerners assumed that people in the North lacked the stomach for a fight. And even if they did fight, they would lose. The boast "One Southerner can lick 20 Yankees!" in *Gone With the Wind,* a popular 1930s book about the Civil War, captured a widespread belief in the pre-war South.

In the North, the common wisdom was that any states that seceded would be unable to stand on their own. Indeed, they would soon come crawling back to the Union. An abolitionist U.S. senator from Massachusetts, Charles Sumner, certainly believed this. He angered many southerners when he said: "My desire is that four or five [southern states] should go out long enough to be completely humbled and chastened and to leave us in control of the government."

This was only one of many insults the widely influential Sumner hurled at the South over the years. Eventually he paid a high price for his boldness. In May 1856 he gave a long speech in the Senate. Essentially, it was an attack on the violent actions of pro-slavery forces in Kansas.

"It is the rape of a virgin Territory, compelling it to the hateful embrace of Slavery!" he shouted. "And it

Charles Sumner of Massachusetts served in the U.S. Senate for more than 20 years.

may be clearly traced to a depraved desire for a new Slave State, hideous offspring of such a crime, in the hope of adding to the power of Slavery in the National Government. Yes, Sir, when the whole world … is rising up to condemn this wrong, making it a hissing to the nations, here in our Republic, force—ay, Sir, FORCE—is openly employed in compelling Kansas to this pollution, and all for the sake of political power."

"JUSTICE BANISHED"

Senator Charles Sumner of Massachusetts delivered in May 1856 his famous "Crime Against Kansas" speech, in which he denounced supporters of slavery in Kansas. Among other things, he said:

"The contest, which, beginning in Kansas, reaches us will be transferred soon from Congress to that broader stage, where every citizen is not only spectator, but actor; and to their judgment I confidently turn. … Let the voters everywhere, while rejoicing in their own rights, help guard the equal rights of distant fellow-citizens. … In the name of the Constitution outraged, of the Laws trampled down, of Justice banished, of Humanity degraded, of Peace destroyed, of Freedom crushed to earth,—and in the name of the Heavenly Father, whose service is perfect freedom, I make this last appeal."

During the speech, Sumner also verbally attacked a fellow senator, South Carolina's Andrew Butler. This was because Butler had helped write the Kansas-Nebraska Act in 1854. In a loud voice, Sumner said Butler had "chosen a mistress to whom he has made his vows"—a prostitute called slavery—who, "though polluted in the sight of the world, is chaste in his sight."

An 1856 political cartoon expressed northern outrage over the attack on Senator Charles Sumner.

Butler got his revenge indirectly two days later. One of his relatives, U.S. Representative Preston Brooks, walked into the Senate chamber and assaulted Sumner. Using a gold-headed wooden cane, Brooks struck him at least 30 times, causing serious head injuries.

Reactions to the attack on Sumner were perhaps predictable. Most northerners were outraged. Most southerners viewed Brooks as a gallant gentleman and a hero. The assault was a potent source of anti-southern sentiment in the North for years. Sumner eventually recovered from his wounds and returned to his post in the Senate after a three-year absence.

★CAMPAIGN OF HYSTERIA

Still more southern hatred for the North was generated by the election campaign of 1860. In addition to the Republican Party's Abraham Lincoln, three other parties entered the presidential race. The Northern Democrats chose Stephen A. Douglas as their candidate. The Southern Democrats chose Vice President John C. Breckinridge. And the Constitutional Union Party chose John Bell.

Despite the large field of candidates, many people in both the North and South felt the Republicans had a strong chance of winning. This caused widespread fear in the South. Southern newspapers frequently reported that Lincoln and other Yankees were up to no good. They were secretly trying to stir up slave rebellions, they said. Already, the papers said, runaway slaves were raping white women and poisoning whites. None of these claims was true. But they added to the growing hysteria that Lincoln's election would bring about the South's downfall. "The designs of the abolitionists," a Texas newspaper said, were to drown the South "in blood and flame" and "force their fair daughters into the embrace" of black men.

Equally frantic was a Georgia newspaper. It insisted that "the South will never submit to such humiliation and degradation as the inauguration of Abraham Lincoln."

As it turned out, Lincoln did win the election. This seemed remarkable to many because he was not even on

ABRAHAM LINCOLN,
REPUBLICAN CANDIDATE FOR PRESIDENT OF THE UNITED STATES.

A patriotic campaign poster supported Lincoln's 1860 candidacy.

the ballot in 10 of the southern states. But he did carry every free state. And he managed to get 180 electoral votes, compared with 72 for Breckinridge, 39 for Bell, and 12 for Douglas. Faced with the Republican victory, most southerners were livid. Many simply refused to accept the idea that a northern antislavery party would be taking control of the national government. They were convinced that their way of life, in many ways built on the institution of slavery, would be destroyed. One Georgian angrily predicted that "in TEN years or less our CHILDREN will be the slaves of negroes."

A South Carolina Baptist preacher, James Furman, and three other men summed up the southern view of the situation in 1860 in a letter to a newspaper:

"The Union of the Southern States with the Northern has been the occasion of serious evils to the

SPREADING FEAR OF LINCOLN

Southern Baptist minister James Furman tried in 1860 to frighten and outrage his fellow citizens about the possibility of Abraham Lincoln's election to the presidency, writing in part:

"Give them the Presidency and its patronage; the millions of money it has to dispense [and] in a few brief years the slave States bordering on the North will have to abandon slavery as the source to them of endless vexation and loss, through the interference of Abolition emissaries, while no new States will be admitted but such as are free—and then, by a vote of Congress, their great idea will be carried out—universal emancipation will be declared. Then every negro in South Carolina, and in every other Southern States, will be his own master; nay, more than that, will be the equal of every one of you. If you are tame enough to submit, Abolition preachers will be at hand to consummate the marriage of your daughters to black husbands!"

Southern States—and is about to become the occasion of boundless disaster and ruin, unless the Southern States apply the remedy. We are not denying that the South has, in common with the North, derived advantages from this Union, particularly in the earlier years of our history. But in the case of the South these advantages are outweighed by the disadvantages to which she has been subject, [and] the mischiefs she must yet experience, unless she takes the remedy in her own hand."

The only way out of their horrifying predicament, many southerners felt, was to secede. Most southern leaders were adamant about leaving the Union and forming their own country. Furman and the others were addressing the citizens of South Carolina, but they gave voice to the feelings of many southerners: "What shall the State do? Shall she remain in a Union thus attended with danger and dishonor, … driven to die like a poisoned rat in its hole? Or shall she assume her unquestionable Independence?"

The South soon chose the latter of these two courses, a decision that would have grave and tragic consequences.

CHAPTER 4
FORMATION OF THE CONFEDERACY

On January 23, 1861, one of the nation's leading Army officers, Robert E. Lee of Virginia, sat down to write a letter. Addressing it to his son, G.W. Custis Lee, he said:

"I can anticipate no greater calamity for the country than a dissolution of the Union. It would be an accumulation of all the evils we complain of, and I am willing to sacrifice everything but honor for its preservation. I hope, therefore, that all constitutional means will be exhausted before there is a resort to force."

As Lee was writing these words, the outcome he dreaded, the breakup of the Union, had already begun. Five southern states had seceded. South Carolina, where dislike for the North was particularly strong, had been the first. It was followed by Alabama, Florida, Georgia, and Mississippi.

On December 20, 1860, the South Carolina Legislature had voted 169 to 0 in favor of secession. Four days later

Writing to his son in January 1861, the future military leader of the Confederacy, Robert E. Lee, expressed his misgivings about the breaking up of the Union:

"Secession is nothing but revolution. The framers of our Constitution never exhausted so much labor, wisdom, and forbearance in its formation, and surrounded it with so many guards and securities, if it was intended to be broken by every member of the Confederacy at will. It was intended for 'perpetual union,' so expressed in the preamble, and for the establishment of a government, not a compact, which can only be dissolved by revolution, or the consent of all the people in convention assembled. It is idle to talk of secession."

they had issued a declaration explaining their reasons for leaving the Union. It said in part that the northern states had "denounced as sinful the institution of slavery; they have permitted open establishment among them of societies, whose avowed object is to disturb the peace. ... They have encouraged and assisted thousands of our slaves to leave their homes. ... A geographical line has been drawn across the Union, and all the States north of that line have united in the election of a man to the high office of President of the United States,

Banner of the 1860 South Carolina secession convention

whose opinions and purposes are hostile to slavery."

When South Carolina seceded, Abraham Lincoln was still the president-elect; he did not become president until March. But he acted quickly anyway, hoping to persuade the southern states to stay in the Union. He wrote to a former congressional colleague, Georgia's Alexander Stephens. Lincoln assured him that he had no intention of interfering with the South's system of slavery. But his effort to calm southern fears was in vain. The secession of slave states continued in January 1861. And on February 1, Texas became the seventh state to leave the Union.

ALABAMA SECEDES

Each state that seceded issued an official document known as an ordinance of secession. This is part of Alabama's, issued January 11, 1861:

"Whereas, the election of Abraham Lincoln and Hannibal Hamlin to the offices of president and vice-president of the United States of America, by a sectional party, avowedly hostile to the domestic institutions and to the peace and security of the people of the State of Alabama ... is a political wrong of so insulting and menacing a character ... therefore: Be it declared and ordained by the people of the State of Alabama, in Convention, assembled, That the State of Alabama now withdraws, and is hereby withdrawn from the Union known as "the United States of America," and henceforth ceases to be one of said United States, and is, and of right ought to be a Sovereign and Independent State."

★MEETING IN MONTGOMERY

Three days later, on February 4, representatives of six of the seceded states met in Montgomery, Alabama. Their goal was to establish a new country, the Confederate States of America. (It was also called the Confederacy.) Spirits were high. In the next few days, as the delegates went about their business, southern poet Henry Timrod honored the new nation with these words:

"At last, we are a nation among nations; and the world shall soon behold in many a distant port another flag unfurled! Now, come what may, whose favor need we court? And, under God, whose thunder need we fear?"

On February 9 the delegates chose Jefferson Davis, a former U.S. senator from Mississippi, to be the president of the Confederacy. He was sworn in nine days later. A clerk who attended the proceedings wrote this description of Davis:

"His stature is tall, nearly six feet; his frame is very slight and seemingly frail; but when he throws back his shoulders he is as straight as an Indian chief. The features of his face are distinctly marked with character; and no one gazing at his profile would doubt for a moment that he beheld more than an ordinary man."

As for Davis' vice president, Alexander Stephens, a colleague later called him "a lean, yellow, care-worn man, his back bent forward almost into a hump, his chest

A portrait of Jefferson Davis by famed photographer Matthew Brady was taken in Washington, D.C., before Davis resigned from the U.S. Senate and became president of the Confederacy.

bowed inward, one shoulder higher than the other … . His face was bony and emaciated, withered and twitching, his scanty hair fell on his shoulders in disorder. His chin was smooth and beardless, his breath short, while his restless eyes blazed with excitement. His voice … was sharp, shrill, and squeaky, and his whole appearance faded, anxious, disappointed, extraordinary—so much so that he passed no one who did not turn and take a second gaze."

The delegates diligently worked on a constitution for the new nation. Overall, it closely resembled the U.S. Constitution, although the Confederacy's president was limited to a single six-year term (compared with the unlimited number of four-year terms then allowed for U.S. presidents).

To no one's surprise, the Confederate Constitution upheld and protected the institution of slavery. Stephens explained his countrymen's views on the subject:

"[The ideas of the founders of the United States] rested upon the assumption of the equality of races. This was an error. … Our new government is founded upon exactly the opposite idea; its foundations are laid, its cornerstone rests, upon the great truth that the negro is not equal to the white man; that slavery subordination to the superior race is his natural and normal condition. This, our new government, is the first, in the history of the world, based upon this great physical, philosophical, and moral truth."

★LINCOLN'S THREAT

Not long after the Confederacy formed, an event occurred that the secessionists saw as a reminder that they had done the right thing. On March 4, 1861, Abraham Lincoln, whom they hated with a passion, was

Abraham Lincoln rode to his inauguration at the Capitol with outgoing President James Buchanan (tipping his hat).

inaugurated. Because so many southerners despised him, government officials worried about his safety at the ceremony. Mounted troops patrolled around the U.S. Capitol, in Washington, D.C. Many sharpshooters were positioned in and around the crowd.

In that crowd was Wilder Dwight, a future infantry officer in the U.S. Army, who later described the event.

President Lincoln spoke to the crowd at his 1861 inauguration in Washington, D.C.

"This morning broke badly, but at noon the sky cleared," he recalled. "When Abraham rose and came forward [to give his inaugural address] and rang out the words 'Fellow-citizens of the United States,' he loomed and grew, and was ugly no longer. I was not very near, but heard him perfectly. … An immense concourse— thousands—stood uncovered and silent, except occasional applause; the voice clear and ringing; the manner very good, often impressive, and even solemn."

In his speech, Lincoln said, "the Union of these States

is perpetual. Perpetuity is implied, if not expressed, in the fundamental law of all national governments. … [Follow] our national Constitution, and the Union will endure forever—it being impossible to destroy it, except by some action not provided for in the instrument itself. … It follows from these views that no State, upon its own mere motion, can lawfully get out of the Union. … I therefore consider that in view of the Constitution and the laws, the Union is unbroken; and to the extent of my ability I shall take care, as the Constitution itself expressly enjoins upon me, that the laws of the Union be faithfully executed in all the States."

The text of the speech Dwight and other eyewitnesses heard that day soon made its way into the South. Most southern leaders saw it as ominous and disturbing. They felt that the new U.S. president had openly threatened the Confederacy by suggesting that its existence was not lawful. In this they were correct.

Most southerners did not want a war with the North, but they feared that Lincoln might resort to force to reunite the Union. If that happened, they were ready. As a leading South Carolinian put it, "If we must pass through the terrible ordeal of War to teach them this lesson, so be it."

CHAPTER 5
ATTACK ON FORT SUMTER

In the weeks after Abraham Lincoln's inauguration, tensions between the North and South continued to increase. Yet for the time being leaders on both sides chose not to start any hostile action. Everyone knew that the onset of war was a strong possibility. Neither side wanted to be seen as the aggressor, though, for fear of seeming to give up the moral high ground. In mobilizing both troops and public opinion, there was a perceived advantage to not being the first side to fire.

Appearing nonaggressive, however, was not going to be easy for either side. Many people in both the North and South demanded that their leaders take a firm stand against the other side. Lincoln had already done so in his inaugural address. In it he had called the southern secessions illegal and promised to uphold the laws of the land. He also had promised to hold onto federal forts in the South that were still under his control.

★WHO WOULD BE FIRST?

On a small island in the harbor of Charleston, South Carolina, stood one of those outposts, Fort Sumter. The thick-walled fortress would soon become the focus of national attention. Lincoln was determined to keep his promise and hold Fort Sumter. In early April the president ordered a group of U.S. ships to take provisions to Fort Sumter. To avoid a major confrontation, he sent a message to the governor of South Carolina. The ships were carrying only food and other supplies, he said, and "no effort to throw in men, arms, or ammunition will be made," except "in case of an attack upon the Fort."

Construction of Fort Sumter in Charleston harbor started in 1829 and continued until 1860.

Southern leaders also tried to avoid appearing aggressive while taking a firm stand at Fort Sumter. Confederate President Davis had earlier claimed that the South had only peaceful intentions. In his inaugural address, he had said:

"[We are] anxious to cultivate peace and commerce with all nations—if we may not hope to avoid war, we may at least expect that posterity will acquit us of having needlessly engaged in it. ... Devoted to agricultural pursuits, [our] chief interest is the export of a commodity required in every manufacturing country [(cotton)]. Our policy is peace, and the freest trade our necessities will permit. ... There can be but little rivalry between us and any manufacturing or navigating community, such as the Northwestern States of the American Union."

Nevertheless, Davis and his advisers agreed that they must not look weak in their dealings with Lincoln and his government. So shortly after the Confederacy formed, they ordered the seizure of all of the Union forts and arsenals in the South. They were unable to take Fort Sumter before Lincoln sent his ships. So on April 9 Davis ordered General P.G.T. Beauregard to secure the fort before the vessels arrived. Beauregard demanded that the facility's senior officer, Major Robert Anderson, surrender. Anderson said no.

This left southern leaders with a difficult choice between two nearly equally negative options. They could back off, which would make them look weak. Or they could take the fort by force. That would make them look strong, but it also carried a high risk of starting a war with the North.

P.G.T. Beauregard was a graduate of the U.S. Military Academy and the first prominent general of the Confederacy.

Another factor that surely played a role in their decision was Virginia. That slave state, which had significant military strength and strategic importance, had not yet joined the Confederacy. Getting it to secede might be worth taking a major risk. As a leading Virginia politician said on April 10, "I tell you, gentlemen, what will put Virginia in the Southern Confederacy in less than an hour [is for the South to] strike a blow."

★LIKE BELCHING VOLCANOES

The blow came just two days later. At 4:30 a.m. on April 12, 1861, Confederate cannons opened fire on Fort Sumter. A prominent Charleston woman, Mary Boykin Chesnut, wrote in her diary that she heard the booming of the cannons. Jumping out of bed, she and her relatives went to the roof to get a better view of the harbor. "The regular roar of the cannon, there it was," she wrote. "And who could tell what each volley accomplished of death and destruction?"

Many others saw the bombardment, which continued

The citizens of Charleston watched the bombing of Fort Sumter.

EXPLOSIONS LIKE EARTHQUAKES

Captain Abner Doubleday, who was the second in command at Fort Sumter, described the fighting on April 12:

"Our firing now became regular, and was answered from the rebel guns which encircled us on the four sides of the pentagon upon which the fort was built. The other side faced the open sea. Showers of balls from ten-inch columbiads [cannons] and forty-two pounders, and shells from thirteen-inch mortars poured into the fort in one incessant stream, causing great flakes of masonry to fall in all directions. When the immense mortar shells, after sailing high in the air, came down in a vertical direction, and buried themselves in the parade ground, their explosion shook the fort like an earthquake."

for 34 hours. Some, like Chesnut, were far away from the fort. "Shell followed shell in quick succession," a reporter for the *Charleston Mercury* wrote. "The harbor seemed to be surrounded with miniature volcanos belching forth fire and smoke." Inside the fort, the officer second in command, Captain Abner Doubleday, fired the first defensive shot. He later described the scene toward the end of the siege, on April 13:

"The roaring and crackling of the flames, the

dense masses of whirling smoke, the bursting of the enemy's shells and our own which were exploding in the burning rooms, the crashing of the shot, and the sound of masonry falling in every direction, made the fort a pandemonium. When at last nothing was left of the building but the blackened walls and smoldering embers, it became painfully evident that an immense amount of damage had been done."

The damage was so great, in fact, that the fort's commander, Major Anderson, had no choice but to surrender. In his official report, he stated with deep regret: "I accepted terms of evacuation offered by General Beauregard [and] marched out of the fort … with colors flying and drums beating."

★PATRIOTISM REIGNS

In the South, reactions to the fight at Fort Sumter were largely patriotic, even among many who had been against secession. Just as some southerners had expected, the event rallied Virginians. The state seceded from the Union and joined the Confederacy April 17, just four days after the fort's surrender. Three more slave states—Arkansas, Tennessee, and North Carolina—did the same the following month.

Personal reactions among southerners were similar.

President John Tyler's death in 1862 was not officially mourned in Washington, D.C., because he was a Confederate.

One of Virginia's most prominent citizens, former U.S. President John Tyler, had earlier argued for preserving the Union. But after his state seceded, he wrote to his wife:

"Well, my dearest one, Virginia has severed her connection with the Northern hive of abolitionists, and takes her stand as a sovereign and independent State. … The die is thus cast, and her future is in the hands of the god of battle. The contest into which we enter is one full of peril, but there is a spirit abroad in Virginia which cannot be crushed until the life of the last man is trampled out."

Love of country was also the order of the day in the North, where most people were outraged that southerners had fired on the American flag. The poet, essayist, and philosopher Ralph Waldo Emerson reported witnessing "a whirlwind of patriotism." Moved by a desire for revenge, he added, "Sometimes gunpowder smells good." In a similar combative spirit, a Rhode Island man told his brother in a letter, "Traitors have begun the conflict, let us continue and end it. Let us settle it now, once and for all."

U.S. government officials, from the president on down, also saw the Confederate attack on Fort Sumter as treason. Lincoln felt that it was further proof that the secessionists were rebels who were violating U.S. law. He called for swift action. "We must settle this question now," he said, "whether in a free government the

The Stars and Stripes became a symbol of the Union after the fall of Fort Sumter.

minority have the right to break up the government whenever they choose."

On April 15 the president requested 75,000 volunteers to suppress the rebellion. He hoped it would take them no more than three months. Like everyone else at the time, though, he was shortsighted. The future held the sad and terrifying reality of years of bloody fighting by millions of soldiers. No one then realized that the most devastating conflict in U.S. history had begun.

TIMELINE

March: Harriet Beecher Stowe's *Uncle Tom's Cabin*, which attacks slavery, is published

May: The Kansas-Nebraska Act passes, allowing settlers of the two new territories to decide whether to allow slavery

July: The Republican Party forms in the North

May: Pro-slavery forces attack the antislavery town of Lawrence, Kansas; northern Senator Charles Sumner is brutally beaten by a southern House member in the U.S. Senate chamber

March: In the Drec Scott case, the U.S. Supreme Court rule that blacks are not U.S. citizens and Congress cannot ban slavery in new territories

October: Abolitionist John Brown raids the U.S. armory at Harpers Ferry, Virginia; he is executed in December

November: Abraham Lincoln is elected president of the United States

February: Seceded states form the Confederate States of America; Jefferson Davis is chosen as president of the Confederacy

ABRAHAM LINCOLN,
REPUBLICAN CANDIDATE FOR PRESIDENT OF THE UNITED STATES.

December: South Carolina secedes from the Union

April: Confederate soldiers attack Fort Sumter, in South Carolina; President Lincoln calls for 75,000 troops to put down the rebellion; Virginia secedes from the Union

GLOSSARY

abolitionist: person who supported the immediate end of slavery

concourse: public space

Confederacy: Southern states that fought against the northern states in the Civil War; also called the Confederate States of America

degradation: ruin, or forcing someone into a ruinous situation

despotism: tyranny, absolute control

dissolution: disbanding, breaking apart

federal: national, or having to do with the U.S. government

inauguration: formal ceremony to swear a person into political office

incompatible: not fitting, unsuitable

menial:	lowly; relating to work requiring little skill
mortar:	cannon with a wide, short barrel designed to fire shells over fortress or city walls
pandemonium:	chaos
rationale:	an excuse
secession:	withdrawal from a nation or group
shell:	metal container filled with gunpowder and fired from a cannon
Union:	the northern and loyal border states that fought against the southern states in the Civil War
vengeance:	revenge, or the act of getting revenge
Yankee:	nickname for a northerner; Union army soldier during the Civil War

ADDITIONAL RESOURCES

FURTHER READING

Bolden, Tonya. *Maritcha: A Nineteenth Century American Girl.* New York: Harry N. Abrams, 2005.

Brownell, Richard. *History's Great Defeats: The Civil War.* San Diego: Lucent Books, 2005.

Hale, Sarah E. *Jefferson Davis and the Confederacy.* Sacramento, Calif.: Cobblestone, 2005.

Haugen, Brenda. *Harriet Beecher Stowe: Author and Advocate.* Minneapolis: Compass Point Books, 2005.

Lester, Julius. *Day of Tears: A Novel in Dialogue.* New York: Jump at the Sun/Hyperion Books for Children, 2005.

Mountjoy, Shane. *The Causes of the Civil War: The Differences Between the North and the South.* New York: Chelsea House, 2009.

INTERNET SITES

Use FactHound to find Internet sites related to this book.

All of the sites on FactHound have been researched by our staff.

Here's all you do:

Visit *www.facthound.com*

Type in this code: 9780756543679

Read all the books in the Civil War series:

A Nation Divided: The Long Road to the Civil War

Bull Run to Gettysburg: Early Battles of the Civil War

North Over South: Final Victory in the Civil War

Reconstruction: Rebuilding America after the Civil War

SELECT BIBLIOGRAPHY

Anderson, Bern. *By Sea and River: The Naval History of the Civil War*. New York: Da Capo, 1989.

Axelrod, Alan. *The War Between the Spies: A History of Espionage During the American Civil War*. New York: Atlantic Monthly Press, 1992.

Basler, Roy P., ed. *The Collected Works of Abraham Lincoln*. New Brunswick, N.J.: Rutgers University Press, 1953–1955.

Bearss, Edwin C. *Fields of Honor*. Washington, D.C.: National Geographic Society, 2006.

Buell, Thomas B. *The Warrior Generals: Combat Leadership in the Civil War*. New York: Crown Publishers, 1997.

Catton, Bruce. *American Heritage New History of the Civil War*. New York: Viking, 2004.

Catton, Bruce. *Gettysburg: The Final Fury*. Garden City, N.Y.: Doubleday, 1974.

Catton, Bruce. *Glory Road: The Bloody Route From Fredericksburg to Gettysburg*. Garden City, N.Y.: Doubleday, 1952.

Catton, Bruce. *Mr. Lincoln's Army*. Garden City, N.Y.: Doubleday, 1951.

Catton, Bruce. *A Stillness at Appomattox*. Garden City, N.Y.: Doubleday, 1953.

Coggins, Jack. *Arms and Equipment of the Civil War*. Mineola, N.Y.: Dover Publications, 2004.

Commager, Henry S., ed. *The Blue and the Gray: The Story of the Civil War as Told by Its Participants*. New York: Bobbs-Merrill, 1991.

Drury, Ian, and Tony Gibbons. *The Civil War Military Machine: Weapons and Tactics of the Union and Confederate Armed Forces*. New York: Smithmark, 1993.

Eicher, David J. *The Longest Night: A Military History of the Civil War*. New York: Simon and Schuster, 2001.

Foote, Shelby. *Stars in Their Courses: The Gettysburg Campaign, June–July 1863*. New York: Modern Library, 1994.

Griffith, Paddy. *Battle Tactics of the Civil War*. New Haven: Yale University Press, 2001.

Hansen, Harry. *The Civil War: A History*. New York: New American Library, 1991.

Hyslop, Stephen G. *Eyewitness to the Civil War: The Complete History From Secession to Reconstruction*. Washington, D.C.: National Geographic, 2006.

Jones, Archer. *Civil War Command and Strategy: The Process of Victory and Defeat*. New York: Free Press, 1992.

Livermore, Mary A. *The Story of My Life: or, The Sunshine and Shadow of Seventy Years*. Hartford, Conn.: A.D. Worthington, 1898.

Marten, James. *Civil War America: Voices from the Home Front*. Santa Barbara, Calif.: ABC-CLIO, 2003.

McPherson, James. *Battle Cry of Freedom: The Civil War Era*. New York: Oxford University Press, 2003.

Morison, Samuel E. *The Oxford History of the American People*. New York: Oxford University Press, 1965.

Oates, Stephen B. *The Whirlwind of War: Voices of the Storm, 1861–1865*. New York: Harper-Collins, 1998.

Post, Lydia M., ed. *Soldiers' Letters from Camp, Battlefield, and Prison*. New York: Bunce and Huntington, 1865.

Zeller, Bob. *The Blue and Gray in Black and White: A History of Civil War Photography*. Westport, Conn.: Praeger, 2005.

SOURCE NOTES

Page 5, line 12: Paul Calore. *The Causes of the Civil War.* Jefferson, N.C.: McFarland, 2008, p. 18.

Page 6, line 1: Ibid., p. 19.

Page 6, line 20: Robert R. Russel. *Economic Aspects of Southern Sectionalism, 1840–1861.* Urbana: University of Illinois Press, 1923, p. 48.

Page 7, line 6: The Inflation Calculator. 4 March 2010. www.westegg.com/inflation/

Page 7, line 8: Herbert Wender. *Southern Commercial Conventions, 1837–1859.* Baltimore: John Hopkins University Press, 1930, p. 85.

Page 8, line 20: Frederick Law Olmsted. *The Cotton Kingdom: A Traveller's Observations on Cotton and Slavery in the American Slave States, 1853–1861.* New York: Da Capo Press, 1996, p. 616.

Page 10, line 2: George Fitzhugh. *Sociology for the South.* (excerpts, 1854.) 4 March 2010. www.faculty.fairfield.edu/faculty/hodgson/ Courses/City/fitzhugh/george.html

Page 11, sidebar, line 4: Ibid.

Page 12, sidebar, line 3: *Discourses of Slavery: The Collected Works of Theodore Parker, Part Five.* Whitefish: Mont.: Kessinger Publishing, 2004, p. 281.

Page 13, line 1: Ibid.

Page 14, line 8: John McCardell. *The Idea of a Southern Nation: Southern Nationalist and Southern Nationalism, 1830–1860.* New York: Norton, 1979, pp. 270–271.

Page 14, line 17: William H. Seward and Frederick William Seward. *William H. Seward: An Autobiography from 1801 to 1834. With a Memoir of his Life and Selections from His Letters.* New York: Derby and Miller, 1891, p. 351.

Page 15, line 20: *The Idea of a Southern Nation: Southern Nationalist and Southern Nationalism, 1830–1860,* p. 134.

Page 16, line 3: James McPherson. *Battle Cry of Freedom: The Civil War Era.* New York: Oxford University Press, 2003, p. 100.

Page 17, sidebar, line 6: Hinton R. Helper. *The Impending Crisis in the South.* New York: A.B. Burdick, 1860, p. 25.

Page 19, line 1: George Fitzhugh. "The Blessings of Slavery," 1857. 4 March 2010. http://occawl online.pearsoned.com/bookbind/pubbooks/ divine5e/medialib/timeline/docs/sources/theme_ primarysources_Slavery_16.html

Page 19, line 13: Samuel E. Morison. *The Oxford History of the American People.* New York: Oxford University Press, 1965, p. 606.

Page 19, line 20: Frederick Douglass Project: In the Classroom: Defending Slavery Packet. 6 April 2010. www.library.rochester.edu/index. cfm?PAGE=2896

Page 21, line 5: James M. McPherson. *Drawn With the Sword: Reflections on the American Civil War.* New York: Oxford University Press, 1996, p. 9.

Page 21, line 11: Lincoln on Slavery. Speech at Peoria, Illinois. 16 Oct. 1854. 4 March 2010. http://academic.udayton.edu/race/02rights/ slave07.htm

Page 23, line 10: *Dred Scott v. Sandford.* FindLaw, Cases and Codes. 4 March 2010. http://caselaw. lp.findlaw.com/scripts/getcase.pl?navby=case& court=us&vol=60&page=393

Page 26, sidebar, line 4: Stephen G. Hyslop. *Eyewitness to the Civil War: The Complete History From Secession to Reconstruction.* Washington, D.C.: National Geographic, 2006, p. 28.

Page 28, line 6: Margaret Mitchell. *Gone With the Wind.* New York: Scribner, 1936, p. 115.

Page 28, line 15: *Eyewitness to the Civil War: The Complete History From Secession to Reconstruction,* p. 36.

Page 28, line 24: Charles Sumner. "The Crime Against Kansas." 19–20 May 1856. 4 March 2010. www.sewanee.edu/faculty/Willis/Civil_War/ documents/Crime.html

Page 30, sidebar, line 5: Ibid.

Page 30, line 5: Ibid.

Page 32, line 17: *Battle Cry of Freedom: The Civil War Era,* p. 229.

Page 32, line 22: Dwight L. Dumond. *The Secession Movement, 1860–1861.* New York: Macmillan, 1931, p. 104.

Page 33, line 10: Michael P. Johnson. *Toward a Patriarchal Republic: The Secession of Georgia.* Baton Rouge: Louisiana State University Press, 1977, p. 47.

Page 34, line 4: James Furman, et al. "Letter to the Citizens of the Greenville District." 22 Nov. 1860. 4 March 2010. http://history.furman.edu/~benson/docs/scgese112260.htm

Page 34, sidebar, line 5: Ibid.

Page 35, line 16: Ibid.

Page 36, line 4: John W. Jones, ed. *Personal Reminiscences, Anecdotes, and Letters of Gen. Robert E. Lee.* New York: D. Appleton, 1875, p. 137.

Page 37, sidebar, line 4: Ibid.

Page 37, line 3: Frank Moore, ed. *The Rebellion Record: A Diary of American Events, with Documents, Narratives, Illustrated Incidents, Poetry, Etc.* New York: G.P. Putnam, 1861, pp. 3–4.

Page 39, sidebar, line 4: Ordinances of Secession: 13 Confederate States of America. 4 March 2010. http://americancivilwar.com/documents/ordinance_secession.html

Page 40, line 8: Paul H. Hayne, ed. *Poems of Henry Timrod.* New York: E.J. Hale & Son, Publishers, 1872, pp. 100–101. 4 March 2010. http://docsouth.unc.edu/southlit/timrod/timrod.html#timr100

Page 40, line 17: John B. Jones. *A Rebel War Clerk's Diary at the Confederate States Capital.* Philadelphia: Lippincott, 1866, p. 36.

Page 40, line 24: Henry S. Commager. *The Blue and the Gray: The Story of the Civil War as Told by Its Participants.* New York: Bobbs-Merrill, 1991, pp. 27–28.

Page 42, line 11: "Cornerstone Speech of Alexander H. Stephens." 4 March 2010. http://teachingamericanhistory.org/library/index.asp?documentprint=76

Page 44, line 1: Elizabeth A.W. Dwight, ed. *The Life and Letters of Wilder Dwight.* Boston: Ticknor and Fields, 1868, p. 33.

Page 44, line 10: "Abraham Lincoln's First Inaugural Address, March 4, 1861." 4 March 2010. http://showcase.netins.net/web/creative/lincoln/speeches/1inaug.htm

Page 45, line 22: Arney R. Childs, ed., *The Private Journal of Henry William Ravenel, 1859–1887.* Columbia: University of South Carolina Press, 1947, p. 66.

Page 47, line 10: Roy P. Basler, ed. *The Collected Works of Abraham Lincoln.* New Brunswick, N.J.: Rutgers University Press, 1953–1955, vol. 4, p. 323.

Page 48, line 6: "Jefferson Davis's Inaugural Address." 4 March 2010. www.civilwarhome.com/davisinauguraladdress.htm

Page 49, line 23: *The Blue and the Gray: The Story of the Civil War as Told by Its Participants,* p. 30.

Page 50, line 7: Rachel F. Seidman, ed. *The Civil War: A History in Documents.* New York: Oxford University Press, 2001, pp. 66–67.

Page 51, sidebar, line 4: Abner Doubleday. *Reminiscences of Forts Sumter And Moultrie in 1860–'61.* New York: Harper & Brothers, 1876. 4 March 2010. www.pddoc.com/skedaddle/articles/sumter_and_moultrie-10.htm#_ftn3

Page 51, line 2: Bruce Catton. *American Heritage New History of the Civil War.* New York: Viking, 2004, p. 54.

Page 51, line 9: *The Blue and the Gray: The Story of the Civil War as Told by Its Participants,* p. 37.

Page 52, line 12: *The War of the Rebellion: A Compilation of the Official Records of the Union and Confederate Armies.* Washington, D.C.: U.S. War Department, 1880, vol. 1, p. 12. 4 March 2010. http://ehistory.osu.edu/osu/sources/recordView.cfm?page=12&dir=001

Page 53, line 10: Lyon G. Tyler. *Letters and Times of the Tylers.* Richmond, Va.: Whittet & Shepperson, 1885, vol. 2, p. 641.

Page 53, line 25: *Oxford History of the American People,* p. 611.

Page 54, sidebar, line 6: *The Blue and the Gray: The Story of the Civil War as Told by Its Participants,* pp. 40–41.

Page 54, line 2: *The Civil War: A History in Documents,* p. 72.

Page 54, line 9: James McPherson, "A Vast Future: Abraham Lincoln and the Struggle for the Fate of Free Government." The Hauenstein Center for Presidential Studies. Grand Valley State University. 29 March 2010. www.gvsu.edu/hauenstein/?id=A7D8FFAD-C031-3A26-FA363AADE9D7C2E9

INDEX

ABOUT THE AUTHOR

Historian and award-winning author Don Nardo has written many books for young people about American history. He lives with his wife, Christine, in Massachusetts.